C000091040

ZOOM FOR TEACHERS
STEP BY STEP GUIDE

A beginner's guide to Zoom 2020 – 2021.
Screenshots, tips, and tricks to become
the best modern teacher.

RICHARD V. ROSS

© Copyright 2020 - All rights reserved.

The content contained within this book may not be reproduced, duplicated or transmitted without direct written permission from the author or the publisher. Under no circumstances will any blame or legal responsibility be held against the publisher, or author, for any damages, reparation, or monetary loss due to the information contained within this book. Either directly or indirectly.

Legal Notice: This book is copyright protected. This book is only for personal use. You cannot amend, distribute, sell, use, quote or paraphrase any part, or the content within this book, without the consent of the author or publisher.

Disclaimer Notice: Please note the information contained within this document is for educational and entertainment purposes only. All effort has been executed to present accurate, up to date, and reliable, complete information. No warranties of any kind are declared or implied. Readers acknowledge that the author is not engaging in the rendering of legal, financial, medical or professional advice. The content within this book has been derived from various sources. Please consult a licensed professional before attempting any techniques outlined in this book.

By reading this document, the reader agrees that under no circumstances is the author responsible for any losses, direct or indirect, which are incurred as a result of the use of information contained within this document, including, but not limited to, errors, omissions, or inaccuracies.

Table Of Contents

Introduction

Zoom Video Communications is an independent information service located in California. It provides video telecommunications and online messaging services through a peer-to-peer software system based in the cloud. It is used for video conferencing, working from home, distance learning, and social connections. Zoom's corporate model relies on delivering a product that is easier to use than alternatives, as well as cost advantages, which involves reducing infrastructure-level hardware expenses and ensuring a strong degree of workforce productivity. It supports a video chatting service, which allows unlimited access to up to a hundred devices at once, with a time limit of forty minutes for free accounts having meetings with five or more members.

Customers have the opportunity to update by subscription to one of their plans, with the maximum allowing up to a thousand persons simultaneously, with no time limit. With the emergence of remote working in this scenario, Zoom's software utilization has seen a significant global rise starting in early 2020. Its software applications have been subject to review by the public and media concerning privacy and security issues. A portion of the Zoom working population is based in China that has given rise to concerns about monitoring and censorship.

Business conferencing apps such as Zoom Rooms are accessible for fifty to one hundred dollars a month. One screen can display up to forty-nine users at once. Zoom has several levels: Basic, Pro, Enterprise, and Business. If you are using Mozilla Firefox or Google Chrome, participants do not have to download the app; they can click on the link and enter from the web page. For Macs, Zoom is not compatible with Safari.

Banking institutions, universities, and other educational departments around the globe use Zoom. Zoom has a record of ten million regular customers, and the app had more than two hundred million active users in March 2020, generating expanded difficulties for the business. The company launched version 5.0 of Zoom in April which resolved a range of privacy and security issues. It includes the default passwords, enhanced authentication, and a meeting place security icon.

You can work remotely on your passion with video conferencing through Zoom. Zoom has features that can help you to organize a meeting formally. Zoom is the best tool for online teaching as it gives whiteboard, annotation, screen sharing, keyboard shortcuts, and much more. Scheduling, joining, starting a conference, and sending invitations to your participants for a video conference is easy with Zoom. It has an assignment and presentations set up as a tool for instructors to involve students in a better learning process. For feedback, there is a polling feature to create a poll and share it with your participants. If you are looking for an application for your meetings and video/audio conferences, try out Zoom as it will provide you with the best features as compared to other tools, including price plans.

Zoom is a simple program that is fun and intuitive to use, yet it holds such a wide array of features that many may slip beneath your notice. This book aims to explain the vast majority of these features to you as they are, at the time writing, from the perspective of a current and active user. If Zoom's user manuals feel too daunting, too technical, or too impersonal, here you will find simple, easy-to-understand step-by-step guides that'll walk you through everything you'll need to know. Before explaining how to install and use the software, however, let us first go over why you should use Zoom software and services.

It is recommended that you begin working with Zoom as soon as possible; we live in an ever-innovative world, where technology is constantly changing and adapting. The sooner you learn this knowledge, the better the foundation you can lay for yourself with the information within.

CHAPTER 1:

Introduction To Zoom Cloud Meeting

WHAT IS ZOOM?

Zoom is an online conferencing application with a central, desktop interface and a smartphone device for users to communicate from any place, with on or off video. Users may decide to record meetings, work on activities, and view or edit on screens with each other, all in one easy-to-use application. Zoom offers high -quality video, audio, and remote screen networking functionality through Windows Phone, Mac devices, iOS, Android,

Blackberry, Zoom, and H.322/SIP room networks. Zoom is typical all along and commonly used in this scenario. The video conferencing system has been the unquestioned pioneer in space throughout the nine years since its establishment.

Zoom is one of the top video conferencing technology systems worldwide in 2020. It helps you to communicate with fellow workers remotely when in-person interactions are not feasible and have become immensely useful for social activities, too. Zoom has been an essential resource for tiny, medium, and broad teams that want to stay in contact and maintain their normal business processes with limited interruption-as as well as being a firm favorite of users.

Yet due to the current scenario, Zoom has lately seen an increase in technical expertise. When more and more people are being driven to work from home and remain safe, Zoom helps them to participate in fun ways to communicate with their peers. Zoom is useful to companies, with the best features the app provides, three options to Zoom, and much more. If you operate a remote squad, Zoom can help you keep in contact with them through its intuitive features of video conferencing.

There is an expense to using the updated function plans from Zoom. When you have the money, invest in an updated package of Zoom. If the response is no, go back to working with your colleagues just the way you are working in free mode.

As a teacher, if you or your learners have a situation that keeps you from meeting the person, Zoom can help keep your class going. Online class meetings, in which everyone is planning to join a Zoom meeting, are one way to create interaction when learners are remote, but Zoom can also be used to assist other learning and teaching situations. So long as a student attendant is on a laptop, they can select a connection to the URL and be taken to a chat with the instructor instantly. This removes slow updates entirely, annoying bonus services, and plenty of boring things. Often people need to upgrade their software or flash player to connect, but that never transforms into an issue that lasts more than two minutes. It is suitable for first-time gatherings and already-off meetings.

Zoom provides different beneficial features for online classes like a whiteboard, screen sharing, screen recording, assignment and presentation setup, etc.

HOW DOES ZOOM WORK?

Zoom enables one-on-one discussion time that can grow into group calls, vocations, training workshops and websites for internal and external audiences, and international video conferences with up to 1,000 participants and up to 49 screen videos. Freebies allow unlimited meetings one by one but limit group time to 40 minutes and 100 participants. The paid plan starts at $ 15 per month per host.

ZOOM PLANS

For the vast majority of users, the free version of Zoom is sufficient. Even if you plan on hosting a meeting of more than three people for longer than forty minutes, a great and comfortable way to work around the free version of Zoom's time limit is to allow a short 5-15 minute break after your first forty minutes expire, and then simply start a new meeting on the same topic thereafter, as you'll find that nothing is preventing you from doing so.

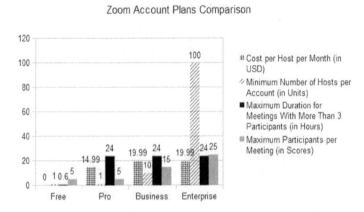

Teachers, students, and entrepreneurs in their early stages can likely get by happily on the free version of Zoom with little trouble.

However, there are another three tiers to be aware of, just in case, they'd be better for your specific situation; *Pro*, *Business*, and *Enterprise*. Pricing plans can be found on Zoom's pricing page.

Pro is sufficient for groups and organizations that have a fairly small number of leaders or managers; for instance, a high school might only have nine teachers assigned to its senior grades, and a local business might have a similarly sized managerial staff. In addition to having all the free version's features, Pro also allows meetings to run up to 24 hours at a time; far longer than most would ever consider holding a meeting outside of Congress. Additionally, you, as a host, are provided 1 GB of storage on Zoom's cloud, making it easier to record and distribute your meetings after the end (as if that wasn't easy enough before). You also have the option to host up to 1,000 participants and gain greater cloud storage space if you're willing to pay a little extra for add-ons. Finally, this is the tier where Zoom's Webinar feature becomes available, and you begin gaining specialized admin tools that let you delegate limited host powers to select non-host participants.

This makes Pro an excellent choice over the free version if you need to reinforce a more serious atmosphere, have long talks with large groups of associates without interruptions, or otherwise, wish to ensure conferences remain orderly through empowered delegation of responsibility.

Business, meanwhile, has all the free and Pro features gives you dedicated customer support (meaning response will be faster and more sensitive to your issues), as well as the ability to weave the brand of your company into the meeting, such as with custom URLs, meeting pages and invitation formats. It requires ten hosts at a minimum, however, each of which will need to pay the monthly subscription, meaning this option is best for large, wealthy organizations who have already established themselves in their field. This is a great option for larger organizations who need a competitive edge, more complex administrative hierarchies during meetings, or a stronger professional image during said meetings through branding.

The *Enterprise* tier, however, should only be considered by extremely large multinational corporations with strong international interest and investment due to its high cost and host requirements. Enterprise's biggest advantage over Business is the sheer size of participants it can host (although similar amounts can be hosted cheaper on lower tiers through add-ons), as well as limitless cloud storage and discounts on Webinar and Zoom Room add-ons, which could end up saving money for exceptionally large businesses if they rely on hosting seminars for hundreds or even thousands of people at a time; although for most organizations, this won't be the case.

DIFFERENCE BETWEEN FREE ZOOM AND PAID ZOOM

There are a couple of differences between the free and compensated Zoom Noting.

FREE CONSUMERS

You can download the Zoom program onto the telephone or your computer and join any assembly using a meeting ID that is furnished. You may opt to disable video or sound before linking. You might make your free Zoom accounts, such as by connecting your Google account, and from there, you can make a meeting, schedule you, combine a meeting, discuss a display, add contacts, etc. Bear in mind you may only be signed into Zoom on one tablet, a single computer, and a single telephone. Zoom has stated that you'll be logged out on the apparatus while logged in to a different device of the same kind if you register into a device.

PAID USERS

You can register and download Zoom on your computer if your system administrator has an Enterprise account, company, or even a Guru, your job email. You need to sync Zoom into your calendar so you can program Zoom meetings and encourage participants that are distant to combine. You're going to require a pc and operate a tablet for attendees along with Zoom Meetings to start the Zoom Meetings if you are establishing a Zoom Room.

You will also require a mic, camera, speaker, a minimum of one HDTV screens to show remote meeting participants, along with an HDMI cable to discuss monitors on a screen, in addition to an online cable to your link, you will also have to get "Zoom Rooms for Conference Room" on the in-room pc and "Zoom Room Controller" to your tablet at the assembly area. So workers can see which assembly rooms are accessible and you may then sync these rooms into the shared calendar of your company.

ZOOM SECURITY UPDATES AND ISSUES

Just like every other software app, Zoom is one of the best video conferencing apps. With an increase in demand, it is unavoidable to have glitches or concerns which can be avoided.

There are several concerns about Zoom, both with guests concerning safety and issues. The business has made many moves to counter such problems and reassure customers about the value of privacy and security.

This includes things like eliminating the assembly ID in this call's title bar; if users discuss screenshots online, the assembly is not subjected to misuse.

SECURITY TIPS.

Be wary of links: Some of the links sent out for one to join a zoom room or meeting might be fraudulent, and when clicked on might expose your computer or mobile phones to malware attack leaking your documents or destroying it fully.

Waiting rooms: It is also advisable to create a waiting room where participants will be before joining the zoom meeting. This minimizes the potential of uninvited participants disrupting your zoom meetings or classes.

Always remember it's been recorded: Try not to do things you would not be proud of and always remember to **either mute or cancel the camera** if you must attend to something else.

Use a work email: I said it earlier on the importance of using a work email instead of a personal one. This is to avoid a leak of any sort in case zoom's network is hacked

Don't fall for fake zoom apps: Very important, because falling for fake zoom apps would mislead you, and you might end up being hacked.

TROUBLESHOOTING

There are common problems associated with using zoom. The most common problems and how to fix them are listed below

Another cause could be that people with computers or telephone speakers might be too close to each other or lastly there might be numerous computers with active audio in the same conference room. The solution to either of these situations is to ask the two people that are too close to each other to move apart. Or one of them would be asked to either leave the audio conference or mute his/her audio on their device.

PROBLEMS ASSOCIATED WITH SHARING A SCREEN:

Sharing of the screen is one of the important features of the Zoom app and a zoom meeting and it is easy by clicking **Share Screen at the bottom of the window.** If you're planning to share your screen during a call and it is not working, it might be because you lack a strong internet connection. Sharing your screen takes up a lot of bandwidth/frequency range. If you are on a call or in a meeting and your screen refuses to share, **turn off your video by clicking the Stop Video button and try starting the video again.**

PROBLEMS WITH RECEIVING EMAIL MESSAGES FROM ZOOM:

Another common problem of the zoom app is not being able to receive confirmatory email messages from Zoom during registration or other notification emails. These usually take between 2 - 30 minutes to arrive and or longer, but if it doesn't arrive, you need to check your spam folder, or you make sure that your email is configured properly.

TIME:

To have more time for your meetings, you can upgrade from the basic plan to other plans.

ZOOM BOMBERS?

The rise in prominence of Zoom must direct the ceremony to be mistreated by web trolls and individuals with time on their hands. Some people have been searching down insecure and public Zoom meetings and allowing themselves, then "bombing" others on the telephone with picture videos, porn, and other inappropriate content. We composed a guide, and there are methods in which you can stop this from occurring, such as procuring your requirements, preventing display sharing, and disabling video. The staff behind Zoom is currently making improvements to keep them secure and to fasten your requirements.

HOW TO STOP ZOOM BOMBS:

The easiest way to avoid getting Zoom bombed is to keep your event private and your invite list small. When creating an event for a large audience, do not share your meeting link directly on social media or multiple platforms.

Default Security Upgrades

Zoom has been upgraded to assist invite users. One of them has become the need for a password as the default option for Zoom meetings. This, together with waiting rooms, ensures that they are allowed in. Another measure is safe and safe.

Zoom Safety Tools

Zoom has made it simple to handle and secure your meetings when they are happening. There is a selection of security tools; now, you can access two or three clicks, such as the capability to lock the assembly as it's begun so that no new people, eliminating participants on the phone, can connect along with disabling chat.

To get the Zoom safety tools, you may click on the safety button, which looks in the window once the phone is currently occurring, or hover over a player to interact with them.

Reporting Other Participants

It is now possible to record participants who are not welcome or are causing difficulty. Now you can send a report to managing abuse of the machine, in addition to removing them on the telephone. This can help to interfere with calls and prevent them. To accomplish this, click on the safety button and click on the report.

Meeting Connector Core Concepts

Zoom supplies service or a public. In the hybrid cloud assistance, you deploy assembly communication servers known inside the internal system of your company. While the meetings have been hosted on your cloud in doing this, meeting and user metadata are handled in the cloud. The Zoom Meeting Connector is done via all assembly traffic such as voice, video, and information sharing. The Zoom Meeting Controller may be deployed onto some other virtualization platform and is packed as an OVF.

Networking Schema

The Meeting Connector utilizes the cloud to the Following solutions: Notification Services for fulfilling invitation notifications on mobile devices and PC

Internet Application Services for meeting and user metadata like login, scheduled assembly list

Cloud Controller for syncing assembly standing

Zoom is an application that you may use to communicate remotely with anyone-either visual or audio-only, or even both when holding live conversations, and it helps you to capture such sessions for playback later. In 2019 over the majority of five hundred companies reportedly used Zoom and hit even higher heights during 2020, claiming three hundred million daily Zoom meeting participants recently.

Zoom is the unquestioned leader in the market when it comes to digital conferencing software. The blend of in-depth functionality, elegant design, and accessible pricing structure allows it a worthy addition to the application framework of every company. Only note to take maximum advantage of all of the services that were provided by Zoom. If you do, you will enjoy all the benefits Zoom has to bring. The program you choose will rely on the team's scale, how much you expect to utilize Zoom, the intent to use the method, and the existing budget.

There were some security issues when the zoom application was launched. With increased demand, the zoom organization takes into account its security issues and updates. The organization has created several movements to counter security issues and reassure users that security and privacy are essential. That involves necessary items like deleting the meeting Identifier from the call's title bar. The organization has announced multiple changes to the program to improve protection credentials.

News for Meetings and Privacy

Zoom's work continues relentlessly aimed at improving the platform, in particular, the one focused on improving privacy and security. Today on the pages of the official blog two interventions: one on end-to-end encryption which, unlike what was announced at first, will be made available to everyone, the other to report some features that are introduced as part of the 90-Day Security Plan launched in early April. The novelties concern the management of accounts as well as meetings to allow advanced control of what happens during a meeting on Zoom.

Here they are:

Added an option that allows administrators to disable the possibility of authentication through email-password pairing forcing users to use SSO (Single Sign-On) or other methods offered by the service for login;

- Administrators can whitelist domains other than their own so that participants can bypass the waiting room and join the meeting directly;
- Administrators can disable the ability for participants to add notes to a shared screen, acting individually, in groups, or collectively;
- You can now apply the "Unmute All" command to activate the microphone to all participants at once in meetings involving fewer than 200 people;
- Webinar organizers and speakers can eliminate questions and comments sent via Q&A and chat during meetings;
- Users and administrators are now able to set how long Zoom can save data such as call logs, recordings, voice messages, and transcripts.

With significant growth in the last few months, also due to the race to adopt smart working, distance learning, and remote communication solutions, Zoom has found itself in a position to expand its workforce by hiring big shots like Alex Stamos (formerly Facebook), Velchamy Sankarlingam (formerly VMware) and Damien Hooper-Campbell (formerly eBay and Google) to improve the quality and reliability of the service offered.

In the same window as the Waiting Room option is the "Lock Meeting" option. Enabling this will guarantee that no further individuals will be able to barge in, no matter what. This can be useful as, by default, both the host and participants alike have the power to Invite new attendees in (under the Participants tab) at any time. Sure, they'd just get caught by the Waiting Room anyway if enabled, but sometimes one can do without that kind of distraction.

Do not think twice about locking the meeting once all intended attendees are in. As a host, you can unlock the meeting at will, if necessary, ensuring that you're simply keeping trolls out, and not alienating intended participants who just happened to get unlucky with time management.

CHAPTER 2:

App Installation

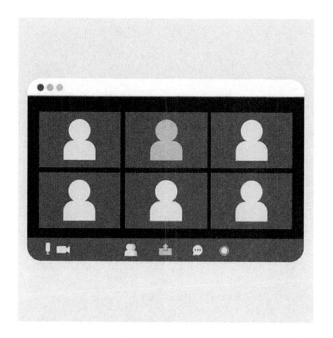

GETTING STARTED WITH ZOOM

*Z*oom can also be accessed through its desktop and mobile application version. The desktop app version can be downloaded on Windows and macOS, and the mobile application can be downloaded on iOS and Android.

While it is possible to access any Zoom meeting without signing up and creating an account, it is advisable to sign up using a Google,

Facebook, or Zoom account if you will use it frequently. This will make it easier to access every time you want to conduct a meeting.

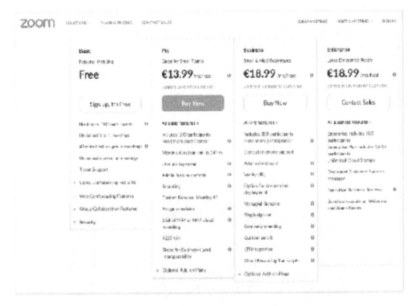

Before we learn about accessing and starting Zoom Meetings, the best way to learn about it is through downloading and installing the Zoom app.

This will simplify its accessibility factor.

Whether you are hosting a meeting or attending as a participant, using Zoom can be extremely effortless once you follow these steps.

DOWNLOAD THE APP:

To download the Zoom App (desktop or mobile app version), you can *click here* to go to the download page.

Follow the steps and once downloaded on your computer, create an account, or log in with your Facebook or Google account.

Upon using a mobile app, an interface like this will pop up as soon as you enter.

For easier understanding, we are assuming that you are using the desktop version of Zoom.

START A NEW MEETING

If you are hosting a meeting, click on the 'New Meeting' option that is represented by the orange icon. You will enter an interface that enables you to change the settings according to your preferences.

AUDIO SETTINGS

First, you will tweak the audio settings. To begin with, find the 'Join Audio' at the bottom-left corner of the window and click the arrow beside it. Click on 'Audio Settings' from the dropdown menu.
A 'Settings' window will pop up

You can always access this window by clicking on the setting icon on the top right part of the screen

Once the window pops up, click on the dropdown list located on the right side of 'Test Speaker' and select the speaker you prefer. You can either choose your headphone jack, your device's speaker, or any other speaker that is linked externally. We would recommend that you wear headphones as it will block out background noise and keep your meeting private if other people are around.

Next, you should check the microphone quality. Click on the dropdown menu on the right side of 'Test Mic.' Depending on the microphone device you are using, select the relevant option. If you have an external microphone connected to your system, the list will display the name. If not, select 'same as the system' to use the device's microphone.

Then, you will check the input level of your microphone and voice quality. Start talking and view the slider besides 'Input Level' as it transitions from red to green. Your audio is stable if you are in the green zone (not too slow and not too loud). Check the box beside 'Automatically adjust microphone volume' to make it easier.

Leave the other settings as they are. You can probably check the box that says 'Join audio by computer when joining a meeting' to access the same setup as soon as you join a call.

VIDEO SETTINGS

Now, we will tweak the video settings. Click on 'Video' located above 'Audio' in the left panel.

The Video Settings box will look like this.

As soon as you click on 'Video', a box appears with a message saying, 'Zoom would like to access the camera.' Click on 'OK.' The black box in this picture will display what is seen by your front-facing camera. This is how the other participants will see you during the call. You can adjust your position and device to provide a clear view.

If you have other devices or webcams attached externally to your video interface, select the device from the dropdown menu beside 'Camera.' Leave the other settings as they are and exit the box.

STOP VIDEO OPTION

Once your audio and video settings are in place, you are good to go. Close the setting page and click on the button "New Meeting" to start a meeting. If you need the call to be just audio, you can select the 'Stop Video' option on the bottom-left corner of the window, as you access the meeting.

INVITE NEW PARTICIPANTS

The next step will involve inviting participants to the call. Select the 'Participants' option on the bottom panel of the window, and then click on "Invite".

You will see a window that looks like this.

You can either invite people from your contact list or via email. The easiest way is to click on 'Copy URL' and send the generated meeting URL with the people you wish to invite. Exit the box. Once you send this URL to the preferred participants, they can easily access the meeting by pasting this URL in their browser. You can also text or send the meeting password to your participants to join the discussion. We will elaborate further on this later in this section.

MANAGE PARTICIPANTS

We will now manage the participants that have permission to access the meeting. Click on 'Participants' on the bottom panel of the main window.

You will see a popup that will display all the participants that have entered the meeting. It will look like this.

If you move your mouse over the participants' names, you can mute a particular participant or mute all of them by selecting 'Mute All' at the bottom. This functionality is extremely useful when a single person is in need to speak or is instructing everyone.

CHAT OPTIONS

Access the 'Chat' option on the bottom of the main window. It will open a popup window. This will allow you to write comments and send messages during the meeting. You can also upload files or photos from your device, Google Drive, or Dropbox by clicking on the file icon.

This is particularly convenient if you want to discuss certain specifications during the meeting, such as presentations, reports, or diagrams. In case you wish to send a private message to a participant you will need to click on "everyone" and select from the list the person that you wish to contact.

RECORD A MEETING

To record the meeting, select 'Record' at the bottom of the main window. As soon as you click the option, you will notice a red pulsing icon in the top-left corner of the window. This signal shows that the meeting is being recorded. The participants will also be aware of the recording as the red icon will be displayed beside your name in the vertical window on the right side of the screen. You can also stop or pause the recording by clicking on the respective buttons beside the recording icon.

To access the recording and choose a particular location to save the recorded data, select 'zoom.us' on the top panel of your window and go to 'Preferences'.

Next, select 'Recording' in the left panel. Click on the list beside 'Store my recordings at,' select 'Choose a new location,' and select the folder or location that will collect all the recordings.

SHARE YOUR SCREEN

To share your screen with other participants, click on the green icon depicting 'Share Screen' at the bottom of the main window.

A window like this will appear.

When this window pops up, you can choose the desktop or screen that you want to share with others.

As soon as you click on 'Share', a window saying 'Allow Zoom to share your screen' will pop up. Click on 'Open System Preferences' and select 'Zoom' from the list.

END THE MEETING

To end the meeting or the exit, select 'End Meeting,' denoted in red in the bottom-right corner. Select 'End Meeting for All' from the pop-up window to end the meeting.

SCHEDULE A MEETING

Now let's try scheduling the next meeting, go to the main page of your app, and click on the icon that says 'Schedule.'

You will see a window like this.

Type the name of the subject, class, or topic of discussion of the meeting in the 'Topic' box. Select the starting and ending date and time of the meeting. Since we are learning the features on the free version of Zoom, you can set only 40 minutes. To increase the duration, go to the official website and buy a subscription plan that offers longer meetings and additional benefits.

Next, select the box beside 'Generate Automatically' under 'Meeting ID' (this should be your preferred option).

Then, generate a password by checking the box beside 'Require meeting password.' Type a password of your choosing and share it with the other participants to give them access to the meeting. By unchecking the box, anyone can access the meeting without a password, so it's always preferable to create a password.

Next, you can select whether you want your video to be on or off during the meeting.

You also have the option to choose whether you want your participants' video to be on or off.

For the audio, select 'Telephone and Computer Audio,' as some of your participants might use their phone and cellular data if they don't have a stable broadband connection.

You can add this schedule reminder on a calendar of your choice. Choose among iCal, Google Calendar, or any other calendar that you use.

Lastly, click on Advanced Options and select your preferred option among 'Enable waiting room' (lets your participants wait before starting the meeting), 'Enable join before host' (lets your participants enter the meeting before you do), 'Mute participants on entry' (mutes all participants until you enter and unmute), and 'Record the meeting automatically on the local computer' (begins recording without selecting the option).

Once you select the appropriate options, click on 'Schedule' and your meeting will be noted on your calendar.

When you open your calendar, you will receive the details regarding the meeting, including the meeting ID, password, and even a mobile tap feature that takes you to the meeting directly if accessed through a cell phone.

Send this auto-generated message containing the meeting details to your desired participants through e-mail or text.

HOMEPAGE OPTIONS

A few more options that can be accessed from the home page (located on the top of the page) include:

- **Chat:** If you have made a few friends on Zoom and added them, they will appear on this Chat on a panel. You can directly chat with them through this option.

- **Meetings:** With this option, you can check all the meetings that you have scheduled for a future date or the ones that have been scheduled for you by someone else. The panel will also show your Personal Meeting ID or PMI. With your PMI, you can use options such as Copy Invitation, Edit, or Join from a Room.

- **Contacts:** You can view your added contacts in this panel, both from your directory and channels.

- **Your profile:** You can change your profile settings by selecting your picture icon on the top-right corner of the home page. This is your avatar. You can add a personal note, set your status as Away, Available, or Do Not Disturb (you can choose the duration), make changes to your profile, and upgrade to the Pro version.

ZOOM MAIN FEATURES

Zoom has many features that make the app desirable and well enough to compete with other video conferencing tools. These features range from the user's ability to share files; share screens while working and record audio and video during meetings. With the increasing demands for Zoom, developers have up their games to ensure users' satisfaction comes first while maintaining the product's long-standing integrity. The following features are common in zoom meetings:

ZOOM ROOM CONTROLLER

To have access to the Zoom control board, your device must be on either of the following OS; apple iPad running on iOS version 8.0 and above; android tablet running OS 4.0 and above, windows tablet running version 10.0.14393 or later, Crestron Mercury.

You need to download the zoom Room controller from the Zoom download page. The following features are accessible with the Zoom Room controller;

- Meet now
- Schedule meeting now with a selected number of participants.
- Contact list display for participants.
- Meeting list
- Display today's meetings list of participants
- Get upcoming meeting alerts.
- Joining a meeting
- Join a meeting using the meeting ID.

Presentation

- Start your meeting while still sharing the screen.
- Set screen sharing duration

Phone

- Switching from a phone Zoom call to a video session.
- Show call history.
- Device settings
- Select microphone
- Select speakers
- Web settings
- Private meeting
- Hide meeting ID.

ZOOM VISITOR CONTROL

The first thing you must ensure is that you have total control of your screen during meetings. You must deploy strategies to keep sanity in the meeting room. This is where visitor control comes in. You do not want a case of Zoom bombing where unwanted visitors are gate crashing your meeting and sharing unsavory contents. You can control the visitor's presence before the meeting and even after the meeting using your *host control bar*. To prevent unnecessary sharing of contents by visitors, make use of the host control bar. Tap the arrow beside the share screen menu to take you to the advanced sharing option. Locate the "who can share screen and choose" the only host." As part of Zoom's effective management of visitors and participants. There are features you must take note of. Follow these steps below to manage visitors effectively:

- Authorize the meeting so that only the invited participants can log in with their email.

- Generate a random Zoom meeting ID for all meetings. This will prevent gatecrashes.
- Remove recalcitrant participants
- Disable video access to your meeting.
- Disallow private chat.
- Use the waiting room.

ZOOM VIRTUAL BACKGROUND

Instead of using the default Zoom background during Zoom meetings, you can make use of virtual backgrounds that can be downloaded online - or from your device pictures or videos. This works better with a green screen and a well-lighted room.

How to enable virtual background in zoom;

- Navigate to the Zoom web as an administrator and click on the Account settings icon.
- Enable the virtual background settings by navigating to the virtual background option.
- Activated.
- How to enable virtual background for group members
- Login to the Zoom web portal as an admin to edit users' group.
- Select the group management icon.
- Tap the name of the group and pick the settings icon.
- Enable the virtual background settings on the meeting tab.
- How to enable virtual background for personal use

- Enter the Zoom Web Portal.

- Access the "my meeting settings icon" if you are the administrator of "meeting settings icon" if you're an ordinary member.

- Enable the virtual background settings on the meeting tab.

To enable a virtual background for the Zoom room.

- Login to the Zoom Web Portal as an administrator.

- Enter the zoom room page and check-in account settings.

- Turn on the virtual background with a green screen.

- You can add more background pictures from your device's library if you want.

- To enable a virtual background on windows.

- Log in to the Zoom desktop client.

- Tap on your profile picture and choose settings.

- Select virtual background

- Toggle on" I have a green screen" if you already have it set up.

- Select your desired virtual background image from the available ones. You can as well add them from your device's gallery.

BREAK OUT ROOMS

The Zoom breakout rooms allow hosts to split zoom sessions into more than one session. It is only the account owner that can have access to this feature.

To enable Zoom breakout rooms for all the members in your group:

- Login into the Zoom web as an administrator that has the privilege to edit groups.
- Access the navigation menu and click User Management and then Group Management.
- Tap the name of the group, then choose the Settings tab.
- Scroll down to the Breakout Room option on the Meeting tab to enable it
- To enable zoom break out room for your personal use.
- Login to the Zoom portal.
- Click Account Management from the navigation menu, and then click on Account Settings (provided that you're the administrator of the account) or Settings (if you are an account member).
- Enable the Breakout Room option on the Meeting tab.

ZOOM SHARE SCREEN

The Zoom share screen is a common feature on zoom for PC, tablets, and mobile devices.

This feature allows participants to share what's on their screen for easy access by the group members.

Co-workers, while working from home, can receive instructions and teach one another using their Zoom share screen.

With this feature, you can see what the other members are doing on their computer screen.

Only that the shared screen can only be done by the host if the account is basic. For premiums accounts, the host and the attendees can both share their screens. The hosts do not necessarily need to grant access before other members can share their screens.

How to share screen on Windows and Mac.

- Locate the share screen icon in the meeting control
- Choose the screen you want to share. You can even share the Microsoft documents screen when opened.
- Tap the share icon to start sharing.
- The share screen will take up all your screen. You can exit the full-screen mode by clicking on the exit full-screen icon.
- While sharing your screen, you can access the following menus;
- Mute or unmute your microphone.
- Start or stop your video.
- If you are the host, you can view or manage the participants.
- Begin a new screen sharing.
- Pause your screen sharing mode
- Invite other participants to join your current meeting.
- Record the meeting to your computer storage or the Zoom Cloud.
- End the meeting at any time you want.
- Turn on the dual monitor option to be able to see both the participants and the screen you're sharing at the same time.

How to share your screen on Android devices:

Sharing screen on Android requires Android 5.0 and later:

- In the meeting Control, click on the share icon.
- A prompt will come up asking you which content you want to share. Choose the content you want to share.
- You can share photos, documents, whiteboards, website addresses, etc.

Sharing screens.

- Click the share icon in the meeting control.
- A list of available sharing options will be displayed. Choose screen.
- Click on "start now" to start.
- You can choose to share anything from your phone's desktop while zoom keeps running in the background.
- You can stop sharing by tapping on stop share at the bottom of your screen.

How to share your screen on iOS:

Needs iOS 11 or higher. You can share photos, iCloud Drive, Dropbox, whiteboard, etc.

You can disallow any of these features from your account settings under the integration menu.

To share content

- Click on share content directly from the meeting control.
- Select the category of content you want to share.

- If it is a document, you want to share, select the document, and choose the document from your Google drive.

To share the screen:

- Select the sharing icon and choose the share screen.

ZOOM WHITEBOARD

The Zoom whiteboard feature will give access to you (the host) and group members to share a virtual whiteboard with annotations. It works best on Zoom for Windows, Zoom for Mac, Linux, iPad, and Android.

Sharing a whiteboard on Windows:

- Tap the share screen icon in the toolbar.
- Select whiteboard
- Choose shares.
- The annotations tools will be displayed. You can show and hide them from the whiteboard option
- Create and switch between pages by using the page control icon located at the bottom right corner of your whiteboard.
- Stop sharing when you are done.

Sharing whiteboard on Android:

- Navigate to the meeting control and click on share.
- Choose the share whiteboard menu.
- Tap the icon that looks like a pen at the extreme left of the screen. This will open the annotation tools for writing and editing.

- Click on the pen icon again when you are done to close annotation.

- Stop sharing.

Sharing whiteboard on iOS: whiteboard only works on iPad for now, and not on iPhone.

- Click on share content available in the meeting control menu.

- Select the whiteboard.

- The annotation tools will come up where you can edit and write texts.

- Tap "stop share" to stop sharing the whiteboard.

ZOOM RECORD MEETING

Tapping the record button at the bottom of your screen can enable you to record a meeting in Zoom. Recording meeting in zoom is good, particularly if there is a particular colleague that should be in the meeting but was unable absent for one reason or another. The individual can always listen to the recording later to understand what has been discussed during the meeting. The organizer of the meeting must give access before you can record the meeting on zoom. If the organizer does not grant access, I am afraid it will be difficult to record such a meeting.

Zoom recording on PC

Tap the recording button at the bottom of your screen to start recording. Tap stop to end recording. The file will be stored as an MP4 on your computer.

Zoom recording on Android and iOS

The same procedure is followed to record in both Android and iPhone devices. You must be on the Pro plan before you have access to the record. Besides, the meeting planner must grant you access.

Open your Zoom app on Android or iPhone to join an ongoing meeting. Click on the three dots at the extreme right corner of your screen. Select record to the cloud (if you are using iPhone) or record (for Android).

You can stop recording when you are done.

ZOOM CHAT

The Zoom chat is a new addition from Zoom to allow business users to chat securely. The chats are stored in local drives or Zoom clouds. Zoom chats add to the complete zoom package where users can access real-time messaging platforms and share business ideas. The Zoom chat is available on both the mobile version and the desktop version. There is a premium account and a free account. Channels on premium accounts can have up to 5000 members or more while the free chat is limited to 500 persons. The Zoom chats are end-to-end encrypted; you do not need to worry about the security of data.

ZOOM REMOTE CONTROL

The Zoom remote control allows participants to control each other's screens while granting access. You can request remote control from the organizer who is sharing his screen. When he grants access, users can have the liberty to control what is happening on their screen.

How to request remote control on windows and Mac:

- Tap the view option drop-down menu to select request remote control.

- After the host grant access, you can then start controlling his screen by tapping inside the screen share.

- To stop remote control, tap the view option drop-down again and choose to give up the remote control.

CHAPTER 3:

Zoom For Teachers

S ymmetric class meetings, through which everybody logs in at a pre-scheduled time to a cloud conferencing program, are one way to create interest and promote collaboration in your complete online courses. Teachers can use a web-conference program in a synchronous session and allow all the students to participate at a pre-scheduled date. The application for video conferencing at the university is Zoom. Zoom may be found on computers, desktops, iPad, smartphones, and even cell devices, enabling students to navigate the class session in several respects.

As a teacher, whether you or your learners have a condition that prevents you from meeting face to face, Zoom will help to keep your class running. Concurrent online class meetings, where everybody is expected to attend a Zoom group, are one way to build interaction while students are far away. Still, Zoom may also be used to help special education and learning situations. Zoom may be used on any device and even workstation phones, allowing students to connect with the team meeting in many ways. You can find tips on planning for your Zoom meetings in this chapter, including gathering students with the conversation, screen editing, polling, non-verbal reviews and breakdown rooms, and supplying your community with open online learning sessions, as well as resources for different teaching scenarios.

PREPARING FOR CLASS

Zoom was developed with creativity. Now, if you make confident important choices and familiarize yourself with the application before welcoming students into an informal conference, it works better. Zoom's free edition can provide you with the best performance and features while holding a Class. Coach the students to have Zoom activated. Students preparing to attend Zoom meetings from a Laptop or computer will also access the application from the Zoom website.

- Get to learn the controls on the server.
- Catch up on managing a quick Zoom meeting.
- Sign up to work out.
- Check the recording and the audio.

- Visit zoom.us/test to confirm the internet, video, and audio connections.

- When there are several meeting participants in the same area, only one person can enter the conference with audio to prevent suggestions.

- Find the source of light.

- Make sure a source of light should be in front of you and not behind you.

SCHEDULE CLASS

Zoom provides a platform for webinars and conferences. All formats help you to communicate with students, although some variations do occur. To pick the style that fits better for you, choose the Zoom flowchart or webinar/meeting comparison chart. Go to the Navigation section to the Zoom feature, press Plan a New Conference and obey the directions.

- Enable your device with the Zoom Windows software.

- Tap at the upper left on "Back".

- Tap "Schedule".

- Enter all related information such as day, year, subject, etc.

- Select your favorite digital calendar (Google Calendar is perfect if you have got Mail or email accounts), and you will be brought to a page with your Zoom connection.

- You may give the connection to your students in the meeting scheduler of your online calendar.

- When applicable, choose regular meetings such that the URL can stay the same over the course. Try to place a positive name on your conferences. Meetings of the course occur inside the platform of the Zoom course.

Recordings can be made accessible automatically via the course page. The course meetings can be separated from other conferences.

Planned meetings often serve as activities for Calendar class participants. For unplanned events, simply use your meeting ID and official Zoom URL. Such gatherings are not going to have the advantages mentioned earlier, so cannot be hosted by someone else.

PLAN ROLES

Assigning specific tasks to the students may be an efficient means of coordinating group practice. Often certain students take too much accountability for the activity of a community, while others may be hesitant to commit to the activities of the group. Assigning responsibilities helps to spread liability among group members and guarantees transparency for the involvement of all students. As students practice various roles, they have the chance to develop a wide range of competencies.

The most needed positions for group work include facilitator, planner, and organizer, timekeeper, and issue manager. You would want to create notes of what it feels like when the job is done well when it is not done well. Ask the students to comment on their perspectives operating in communities in writing or solving issues. Students might still have suggestions for different assigned positions. When you appoint someone else to handle facets of digital rooms, you will have a less challenging classroom managerial experience. Try requesting one supervisor or student to track the conversation and one to assist their peers with difficulties with technology. Formal identification of alternate hosts may also be created. This way, you will focus on giving lectures and offer some additional technical skills to the students.

ENHANCE STUDENT'S SENSE OF COMMUNITY

If everybody reveals their faces through their webcam, the feeling of presence is strengthened. Suggest asking students to click on film as a core component of attendance, because if you can see them, it becomes simpler to communicate with the class, so students are more willing to pay care because they realize they are on display. Train students even about how to turn to the view of the Gallery (this is the perspective where everybody is equally accessible to one another).

Suggestions to connect with your students:
- Make eye contact with the camera.
- Mute mics in case you do not participate.
- Find the illumination! Make sure a bright light is in front of you and not behind you.
- Talk in a conversational way-you does not need to talk up.
- Read on to operate a seamless meeting in Zoom for further information.

A good sense of community can boost the class online and lead to student achievement. The culture can be improved if you take action to keep it protected from harassment or disturbance. A few approaches to meet such targets are here:

Introduce yourself with the safe Zoom Meetings setups and guidance.

Using the regional meeting configuration and in-meeting guidelines to ensure the class is attended only by enrolled learners and invited visitors.

MANAGE TECHNICAL PROBLEMS

For every video conferencing program, the three most important technological problems are:

- Members could not see.
- Members could not hear.
- External noise and mic problems.

You can overcome technical issues by hosting an online training meeting for reduced stakes, with the primary aim of signing in, troubleshooting technological issues, and getting accustomed to the Zoom application. Get in your meeting early enough to sort out technical problems. Provide a contingency strategy in case of unknown complications or challenges. Students are informed of the backup plan in advance so that if technical issues arise, they can stay on task.

Know how to address these problems by troubleshooting issues. Try communicating with your community the Participant's Guide for enhancing Your Zoom Performance. It is recommended to host an online discussion experience with low-stakes introductory meetings, whose primary purpose is to have an entire team login, diagnose problems, technical issues, and get used to Zoom functionality.

CREATE A TEACHING AGENDA

Prepare for a simultaneous training session online much as you would prepare for an in-person meeting. Discuss the plan with students in advance, and students do have a good understanding of how the curriculum is going to proceed, what is going to be discussed and the events they are going to compete in. Periodically review web behavior and student aspirations or recommend providing the "**good management**" guide detailing goals.

Plan for a concurrent session of the course much as you would prepare for knowledge gives the lesson.

Here is a testing agenda for a simultaneous sixty-minute instructor meeting to share your agenda with students in advance, so they know what is coming:

- Make students reflect on a problem before joining the digital classroom and write their answers on the whiteboard.

- Using the polling method to ask a question that includes and decides personal significance for the Mini-reading subject.

- Link computer launches PowerPoint and offers mini-readings. To mark the PowerPoint slides, use the Annotation functionality in Zoom.

- Render the survey issue provisionally.

- Assign students to separate breakout spaces, chat for ten minutes, and develop a shared Google Report.

- Ask each party to appoint a delegate, to sum up, the main points of their debate.

- Ask students to support conversation if they are always puzzled.

- Clear up misunderstandings found in the muddiest point conversation.

- Summarize the session's tasks, set goals for the follow-up events, and achieve them.

RECORD YOUR CLASS

If somebody has a technological problem, you can offer them further access to the course work. You should report the class session to counter this. Record on the web, not on your desktop: Recording in the cloud is easy because you will access both a video URL and an online transcribed clip. Zoom recordings do not have a quota, so records of meetings sessions using Zoom can surface only a few hours.

Begin recording in the appropriate style: Once you start recording, the recording interface is focused on your vision. Note to swap presentations and turn to an active speaking view rather than a gallery (or do not use the camera or anything), or you will be overlaid in the clip over the upper right corner.

While recording your class, keep in mind certain things;

- Let the students know that you will be recording the class.

- Give students a choice to silence their audio when filming and switching off their camera.

- When meetings are captured in the cloud, and you use a module, the recordings can be located right in the PC.

- Such records could be done to specific preservation procedures than other documentation of class sessions.

- For advice about where to place the recordings, and how to show them to your students, contact your local university development help.

SPECIFIC TEACHING SCENARIO

If you are the one who is assigned to take notes (a great practice in usability), you should create closed captions, enabling you to translate what is being said in real-time. Zoom conveniently combines with services such as Play Media when you require live annotations. Prices for such a provision are not directly provided. Many students cannot see the graphic presentation or make sense of it as you wish. Take the habit of conceptually describing what happens on the screen.

SMALL-GROUP DISCUSSIONS

Screen sharing may be used to collaborate with a person or group of students to discuss the course. Approving remote screen monitoring enables one to take possession of the interactive program of the other, which allows the remote device to browse, enter code, etc. Remember that your Breakout Room configuration will be deactivated when remote screen control is available. Collaborative problem sharing and brainstorming are effective to annotate a whiteboard, using the virtual whiteboard application digitally. Allow everyone to annotate on the same platform in the session to express ideas and methods for solving problems. A screen is handwriting support.

You can use the high-quality audio and footage from Zoom to easily have a conversation with a person or student community. Share documents or something else on your device conveniently via sharing a screen to support your discussion in an online class. The waiting room presents you with a single Zoom user ID and the option to invite-only chosen individuals to the conversation. In your waiting area, you can even set up a personalized greeting that lets students realize you will be seeing them early. Start small discussions when most students join your meeting.

ZOOM ASSIGNMENT SETUP

Instructors have the option to set up a Task or Debate Board in all courses and encourage students to download or submit a file. Large recording files may take up a lot of room in the course, or the submitting region of the student's program. There is a specific feature for Zoom videos that will guarantee students can reduce their number of files to a minimum. The application is recognized as the Media Record/Upload method. It would require students to upload five hundred Megabytes files without restricting either the course or the students. Setting up an Assignment or Discussion forum post with these resources, and having the students know the correct way to

ZOOM FOR TEACHERS STEP BY STEP GUIDE

apply is particularly crucial for the teacher. Do not search the "Data Uploads" box when setting up the assignment because the students would use up much of the course room. Alternatively, you can allow the "Record/Upload Files" feature to avoid massive uploads of files for your task. If you duplicate Assignments from previous classes, you will still need to change them.

UPLOAD ASSIGNMENT ON ZOOM

When you have chosen the "File on this Device" choice to document your presentation, using the steps below to transfer your file to an Assignment. Your professor will provide the task that is designed to take a Zoom recording. You should not add a Zoom link to a request that has a click "Link Upload".

- Select "Send Application" to start Notification.
- Select "Media track/Upload".
- Choose the tab "Upload files" then press the button "Download video file".
- Using the Zoom Data File on your Windows.
- Select on "Deliver Assignment".

ENGAGING STUDENTS USING DIFFERENT FEATURES

No one likes sitting through a normal classroom lecture for sixty minutes, and the reality that you have all the teachers there and present does not influence such a class session structure. You may use the Zoom functions to direct various kinds of interactive tasks. Such tasks provide flexibility to break up a long-class session and provide diverse forms of communicating themselves.

CHAT

Using the chat platform will promote interaction by encouraging students to connect, rather than only listen, with the live operation. Also, Chat has advantages over conventional classrooms: Get vast quantities of replies to a question right away, then use those answers in need or save them for later. See just where the students feel on a specific topic of discussion, advising them who to contact next.

Think about when, or where to allow students to talk. Are you happy with feedback during the class in chat, for example, or just at specific points? If you have a supervisor that can delete comments, you can require students to chat on an ongoing basis; otherwise, you can promote its usage at distinct times. Chat enables posts to be submitted to the whole community or another user. If you want to hold the record, you may access the complete chat history of the lesson.

For students, chatting can be unbearable. It is advised that you provide this form of interaction as an alternative, but not all students need it. Even chat can be challenging to track when you are still attempting to lecture. Provide a student or supervisor supervising the conversation so that you can concentrate on teaching.

Recreate live posting on twitter of guest lectures as a way to gather questions and answer them at the end of the meeting.

Select one student to track the conversation when they come in and to compile queries. Create a simulated team, where a selected community of students collaborates to solve a question or address an issue. The other students respond via the chat communications channel to contributions with their fellow students.

Invite students to record questions as small groups during your classes and invite one student to address them for community discussion.

SCREEN SHARING AND ANNOTATION

Zoom provides simple annotation resources that can be used to direct or illustrate an idea to students. Use such resources by choosing the choice Annotate while viewing the display. Computer annotations were not open to those of screen readers. When you are utilizing this tool, make sure to follow best practices for open presentation: explain what you are doing when you are doing it (for example, "drawing a huge red ring around the registration form on this new website").

Sharing the screens is very important to show to your students to enhance your teaching skills and your students' learning ability. You will share the computer screen with anyone at the Zoom meeting using this icon of screen sharing. Sharing a screen with Zoom is simple; all you have to do is press on the "Share Screen" link at the bottom of your conference. You will then press on the device you would like to display. Its modern technology and infinite functionality which help students in their classroom are becoming more efficient and imaginative.

POLLING

Engagement in a virtual class is a core aspect of student performance. Try integrating polling functionality into difficult concepts to improve student interest with your online course. Polling enables students to share their experiences and communicate with each other, and often tells coordinators about the students in the class and encourages them to set the stage for a positive segment further. For an online course, surveys are an essential method, as they can:

- Link students in the classroom so that they can express their views on different topics.
- Be more interactive in introducing a topic or action.
- Give useful information on the readiness and progress of the students.
- Help guide and concentrate students on their education.

Polls are simple to set up and then use and will bring value to an online course. A teacher is provided with several ways to incorporate this practice into Zoom. Set up polling ahead of time and start them in your class meeting.

NON-VERBAL FEEDBACK

Significant feedback on assignments promotes analytical thought, proactive practice, and establishes relationships between teacher and student, which are vital in an online setting. Although feedback helps evaluation, improvement, and enhancement of results, it often improves student enthusiasm when they believe that the teacher is involved in their progress.

To encourage students to connect with the coaching staff without disturbing the class, enable the non-verbal input function for your meetings. Check-in with the students regularly to answer any non-verbal suggestions. This app also helps you to handle vocal input, since students will be told to use the "lift hand" function to signal when they want to talk. Need to make students quiet before you order them to remove outside input from the room.

BREAKOUT ROOMS

Breakout Rooms encourage you to divide the meeting into several meetings, in a live classroom environment, comparable to community breakout sessions. Students should create their social groups and would promote further interaction. You will use the versatility of the breakout rooms in Zoom to help students perform collective learning. As the teacher, when it is time to rebuild, you can enter the breakout rooms, relay notices to the breakdown rooms, and finish the breakdown session.

ZOOM INDIVIDUAL PRESENTATION SETUP

Allow the time to customize the external atmosphere before you present a specific presentation. If necessary, prepare a document of the conversation with a microphone because such microphones will eliminate noise not coming from three to five meters away from the mouthpiece. Use a space where you can shut the door or not be disrupted while minimizing audio from elsewhere in the room. Tiled rooms are recommended over wooden floors to lessen the noise effect in your audiotape. When you capture the video image, sunlight will be coming from in front of you and never behind you to stop putting shadows on your eyes.

One or two crane lamps are lined up behind the screen monitor, and you will be doing this conveniently facing it. Your backdrop should be fascinating but not intrusive, and it does not include a window if the window has both shutters and curtains to obstruct the light. While capturing, mute the mobile phones, email updates, text messages/chats, and other electronic signals. Many vibratory alerts from cell phones are visible when using the smartphone microphone, so you may need to put your mobile phone on a comforter or smooth surface to minimize this

PROFESSIONAL AND PERSONAL DISTANCE

In an ideal case, all communication between the student and teacher would take place using school property, such as an LMS. In reality, not all school districts have an LMS that can accommodate video and audio communication. Furthermore, not all LMS have appropriate "push" notification or message sending capabilities. If the message is purely confined to the LMS and the student never logs into the LMS system, he or she will never see the message.

On the other hand, if you interjected your feedback on last night's homework question into a student's social media feed, you might have a better chance of reaching the student in a timely fashion.

However, this breaches the distinction between personal and professional communication. Text messages and messaging services such as WhatsApp can also breach this divide.

Some students and teachers can easily separate a school-based discussion in one chat window from a casual conversation in a neighboring chat window. Others cannot. Reduce the risk of unwanted and inappropriate communication by making it clear that the communication you use is for professional purposes.

Email is the middle ground because email is frequently used for both personal and professional communication. Using school resources, such as the LMS or school email address would be preferred.

However, if you must use common platforms such as Gmail or Discord, you can still try to delineate the professional nature of the communication channel. Don't use your personal Gmail address. Obtain a new one that relates to school. Johnnydoe@gmail.com sounds like a personal address. MrDoe-MercyHigh@gmail.com marks itself as a school-centric email address. You can similarly name Discord channels or other meeting places to remind everyone about the nature of the communication.

The content of your messages can also breach the personal-professional divide. Some teachers like to build rapport with students with casual conversations, jokes, and a more approachable personality. That's great, and I'm not saying that you can't do that, but you need to remind the students that they are communicating with you for education. When you are physically within a classroom surrounded by other students, the context is obvious. Teachers stand at the head of the class. Students sit in desks. All communication takes place within this context. When a student is texting you while reclining on a sofa in his living room, context can be lost easily.

Students engage in inappropriate behavior, such as asking a teacher on a date, but the context of a classroom surrounded by other students meant that the behavior could be defused easily. Everyone, including the instigating student, understood the absurdity of his behavior. A joke, however inappropriate on the student's behalf, was more likely to remain a joke because the context of the situation was inescapable. Don't let your students or you lose the context. You can achieve this by making sure the context of your online communication is always distinct from personal and casual communication. Even something as small as using proper grammar and punctuation in your messages can help with this. On the other hand, some educators advise that you should use smiley faces and emoticons to connect better with your students. Every situation is different, and what's appropriate in one situation might not be in another. What works in a college course doesn't necessarily work in elementary school.

But in all situations, I encourage you to put as much distance between your professional and personal communication channels as you reasonably can, however, you view and define those terms. These demarcations should also be apparent to the students, and by doing so, you set up clearly defined norms, which is the subject of the next section.

A final suggestion is that group meetings are usually more professional than one-on-one meetings. There are accountability and a common agenda. Instead of meeting with students individually online, consider setting up small groups of appointments or office hours for more personalized, yet professional, discussions, and feedback.

DEFINE A PRIMARY COMMUNICATION CHANNEL

Consider what happens if a student has a question about a homework assignment during the evening. In a traditional classroom setting, student-teacher interaction takes place during the school day. Most, but not all, students would not even think to call or email their teacher late at night over a difficult homework question.

However, what happens in a distance learning environment? In an asynchronous setting, students access pre-recorded videos and download assignments at their schedule. There's no context of "school hours" outside what their parents might enforce. In that case, a student might be more inclined to send an email at midnight, when he's working on his assignment. What's the expectation for you, the teacher? Are you supposed to reply to this email as soon as you see it? Within one hour? By the next working day—when the student may have moved on to something else, reducing the quality of the engagement?

It's impossible to be available for twenty-four hours. You're a teacher, not an emergency room doctor. Define clear communication channels between yourself and your students, and make sure your students follow those channels. If students disregard your guidelines, remind them, and nudge them back into the norms. Stand by the lines you draw; you're not helping your students by encouraging undisciplined violation of rules. If your course materials are primarily asynchronous, it would make sense to set up office hours, daily or weekly as it makes sense for you and your students. Do keep in mind that older students have multiple classes and multiple teachers, all with competing workloads. An in-person high school schedule automatically makes sure there are no time conflicts between courses. In the case of a sudden switch to distance learning, the history teacher may have reserved Wednesday mornings, the math teachers want to hold office hours at one in the afternoon each day, and the music teacher is experimenting with a virtual orchestra on Friday mornings. Consult your students. Offer more than the minimum office hours so that they have a choice of which session to attend in case of conflicts. Another approach is to have students register in advance for time slots. This prevents you from wasting time sitting around if no one is going to show up. I would discourage one-on-one video chats, but you can instead have group signups, or consolidate the time slots so that three to four people show up for them. Even if you offer synchronous class time, students may still have questions outside the allotted hours. In that case, designate a primary channel of communication. Email is the obvious choice, with an LMS-integrated messaging, or at least a professional email, being preferable as described earlier in this book. Set clear expectations. Will you reply to emails between nine in the morning and five in the evening? Tell the students upfront what they can expect. If the email arrives after five in the evening, let them know that you are unlikely to respond to it until the next morning. And if you have homework deadlines, be sure to include the specific time on the due date. Such expectations apply to students, too. If you email a student, what happens if he doesn't reply, or replies after three days?

You can make it clear from the outset that you expect all emails to be professionally handled, which means replies within one day at most. You could even use emails to evaluate a participation grade, with deadlines for replies. Compared to normal email use, that might sound strict, but let's be realistic. If you sent an email to thirty responsible, working adults asking for feedback within one day, how many would reply on time? Now consider the same scenario for young students at home with little accountability.

That brings us to the next section about accountability.

DEFINE CLEAR NORMS

Norms, or standards of behavior, in a classroom are clear to most students and teachers because of years of repeated practice:

- Students sit at desks. Teachers sit or stand at the front.
- If a student wants to speak or has a question, he raises his hand. While the teacher is speaking, students are expected to be quiet. This can, of course, change if the teacher opens the class up to discussion or if the teaching style facilitates casual and frequent dialogue.
- If a student wants to use the restroom, he signs out or takes a hall pass specifically for that purpose. Only one student can leave the class in this fashion at a time.

- Shouting, using a phone, throwing things—these are generally prohibited.
- Some teachers may allow drinking or food during class. In elementary schools, a specific snack or break time may be set aside.
- Students refer to teachers by their last names.
- Students don't curse, use obscenities, or slang when speaking in class.
- Students dress appropriately, defined by the school dress code or the need to be non-distracting to other students.

The above list is hardly exhaustive or uniform among classrooms, but it represents some common standards of behavior.

When switching to an online environment, there can be confusion about the norms. This confusion is exacerbated if casual and professional communication channels are intermingled.

As an example, imagine that the teacher creates a public social media profile to distribute course materials. A common use case is to upload videos to YouTube. What are the norms for student behavior in this case? Will the teacher moderate the comments below the video? If a student makes an inappropriate remark, will the teacher seek disciplinary action? What if a student shares a link in the comments to a site that you haven't vetted? What if a student asks a question—should you, the teacher, be expected to reply to the YouTube comment immediately? What if you never see the comment?

Another example is using a group webcam sharing technology such as Zoom. Who is allowed to type into the common chat area, and when? Who is allowed to make voice comments, and when? Do students always need to show their faces on the camera? What if a student needs to leave during the middle of class? What if a student is not paying attention?

Proper classroom behavior in an online setting can be unclear to both your students and you. If there's a mismatch of expectations, that can ruin the quality of engagement.

Here are some suggestions for setting up norms for distance learning engagement.

GREATER DISTANCE REQUIRES GREATER ACCOUNTABILITY

Fostering engagement with your students is critical to success in distance learning, but there's one big caveat: Your students have to show up for you to engage with them.

There's a world of difference for accountability in distance learning versus in-person classes, which tends to have a very negative effect on education if you don't take special care to address this issue. While the most disciplined and motivated students may perform the same, or even better, in an online teaching environment, most students will face some, if not substantial, difficulties.

In an asynchronous teaching situation, other than tracking logins and grading submitted assignments, it's nearly impossible to know if students are watching recorded lectures at all or fast-forwarding to the end. Some districts use draconian measures such as requiring all personal laptops to have monitoring software during coursework, in some cases including webcam monitoring. However, even such severe measures are trivial to work around. It's not difficult to be watching a different video on a phone set next to the laptop.

It's nearly impossible to instill classroom discipline to the same degree in an online setting as a physical classroom. Sending someone to after-school detention or even suspending them isn't quite the same when the student is already staying at home. The line between truancy and poor performance also blurs. What's to keep an unmotivated student from logging in and ignoring the coursework if he isn't concerned with grades?

Parental oversight can go a long way in making sure that students are held accountable. Sending home a set of guidelines or expectations for the distance learning environment, or better yet, having a parent or guardian login to the LMS to provide an additional layer of oversight can be quite helpful at times. However, expect a wide range of commitment levels from parents, not just the students. In the end, there's little that can be done beyond a parent-teacher phone call or meeting to address truancy or discipline issues, other than warning of a failing grade. Be sure to follow all district guidelines on confidentiality and privacy for any parent-teacher communications.

Still, it's a good idea to involve the parents, even more so than you might ordinarily, for an online teaching module, particularly with younger students. You'll want to make sure that everyone has access to adequate equipment and resources. If there are special circumstances, like a noisy home environment with small toddlers, you'll want to work with the parents, and possibly the district, in finding a suitable solution, whether that involves lending equipment or providing isolated classrooms or library space for students in need. Beyond parental involvement, grades are the primary form of accountability. For a physical classroom, homework assignments and exam scores are the most common components of a grade, with the occasional participation points and group projects added into the mix. The social constructs and disciplinary responses within a physical classroom are typically enough to enforce model behavior in the majority of students.

Don't expect the same in a virtual classroom. Even many adults struggle to adapt to a work-from-home environment. Create more leverage points for grading and other kinds of rewards. Create more accountability, as we'll describe in the next section.

LIVE STREAM A MEETING WITH ZOOM

SETTING UP LIVE STREAMS

An option for holding massive virtual public events, webinars allow between 100-10,000 view-only participants. This means they can use the chat feature to ask questions if enabled but cannot speak directly and aren't as likely to interact with one another. Depending on chat settings, they may not interact with one another at all. You can have a further 100 panelists on top of this - participants who can speak and use their cameras. Webinars are only available to those with a Pro account or higher who have also purchased the Webinar add-on and can only be used by users who have been licensed. You can then, as the account Owner or Admin, assign the add-on to one of your Account users by signing into Zoom's website, then going to "User Management," then to "Users." Click "Edit" at the end of the Username that you wish to assign the license to, then ensure that "Licensed," then "Webinar" is ticked. Then, click "Save."

To set up a webinar, stay logged into the Zoom website, then go to "Webinars," then "Schedule a Webinar." You'll see the process is much like scheduling a meeting, and you'll even see the option to make your webinars recurring. By this point, you should be able to choose the options you want on or off without hand-holding.

Note that if you require participants to register, you can have them answer a pre-meeting questionnaire. You can do this via the Zoom web portal by going Webinars > Invitations > Approval > Edit, then navigating to the "Questions" and "Custom Questions" tabs. Do not forget to save when you're done. You can add your panelists while under "Invitations" too, by clicking on its own "Edit" button. Non-panelists are invited simply through the "Copy the invitation" and "Email me the invitation" options next to your webinar's name.

Once your webinar is set up, you can start it via Zoom's website, or your Zoom app through logging in, going under "Meetings," then finding your webinar and clicking "Start."

Aside from the addition of panelists and the potentially huge attendee sizes, Webinars have many of the features present in normal Zoom meetings. Consider using Mute All, Co-Hosts, and participant size add-ons as alternatives if you aren't sure a Webinar is what you need for your strategy. Note that there are no Reactions, Waiting Room, or File Transfer features in a Zoom webinar.

LIVE STREAMS

Live streaming is a feature that lets your Zoom meeting broadcast in real-time to other media platforms, allowing you to reach audiences on YouTube, Facebook, and more. Live streams can be enabled for both regular meetings and webinars, but again require an account of Pro or higher. To ensure live-streaming has been enabled for you, as an admin you can log onto Zoom's website and go Account Management > Account Settings > In Meeting (Advanced) > "Allow live-streaming the meetings."

Then, check the streaming services you wish to be able to use. For webinars, this can be done via the Account Management > Webinar Settings > Edit. If you wish to use a custom streaming service, be sure to check that option, then provide a Stream URL, a Page URL, and a Stream Key where you're prompted for instructions, so hosts will be able to use that custom option should they wish.

Then, when you wish to host a live-streaming meeting, log into Zoom's website. Click on "Meetings." Then, schedule a new meeting. When you click "Save," investigate the Advanced Options that pop up. You'll see which platforms your meeting will be able to stream to, as well as for instructions for how to commence live streaming in your Zoom app. If you wish to use a custom service, click on "configure live stream settings" now. This will let you fill in the

Stream URL, Page URL, and Stream Key for your customer service now, so you won't need to worry about doing so when trying to live stream mid-meeting.

TIPS FOR LIVE STREAM ZOOM

There are a few things you can do to ensure you have the best experience when incorporating video conferencing into your workflow.

PROPER LIGHTING

It's important to ensure that your location is properly lit when using video communication to ensure your video recipient can see you. It can involve getting away from windows that can induce backlighting whether they're behind you or shadows are intense. Likewise, low light can be a problem, so be sure to have overhead lighting or a handy lamp to fight low sunlight.

INVEST IN THE BEST QUALITY HEADPHONES

In a quiet home environment, depending on your computer speakers and microphone capability may be adequate. This might not always be the case in a large office, coworking room, even whether you have to answer a call when out and about. There are plenty of decent ones on the market and that could be the difference between a smooth video chat and a boring one where everyone needs to repeat themselves over and over again.

PRELIMINARY TROUBLESHOOTING

Have a couple of tried and tested troubleshooting solutions available as problems inevitably emerge. Your Internet protection tools, for example, could block your webcam or audio. Or the headphones which you use may not produce the best quality of audio. Know where your preferences for configurations are for applications that you use to search for quick fixes such as unselecting options that obstruct access to audio or webcams.

STILL HAVE RIGHT TO BACK UP

Although technological requirements are increasingly growing, technology still has a way to fail right as its most important. For those who cannot use their machines for any purpose, Zoom helps you to dial into video calls from a landline. You may also have other favored forms of backup.

CHAPTER 4:

How To Use Zoom For Webinars

M ost Zoom users will be using the service for meetings but there will be other users who will use the webinar feature of Zoom for personal or business reasons. Webinars are invaluable in gathering a group of people that can't be together for the sake of workshops and impromptu meetings. It makes it possible for such activities to occur like they were all there.

ZOOM HAS TAKEN THE LEAD IN MAKING THESE ACTIVITIES POSSIBLE

It's noteworthy to understand what a webinar is; A Webinar refers to an online event where a speaker or more addresses a large audience on a particular topic of interest. Webinars give the host a level of control over such meetings via enhanced features.

Zoom webinar services can accommodate a 100-10,000 person audience. To activate your webinar service, you have to choose any of the zoom plans that you can afford and buy the webinar add-on to be able to subscribe to the webinar services. The zoom plan subscribed to determines the number of people that can attend the meeting

Having been licensed by Zoom, you can proceed to put your webinar in shape

Highlight the Webinar option in the Personal section of the Zoom icon, schedule a webinar button will pop up, select it

After that, fill in the topic for the webinar, elucidate what the webinar would entail, and signify when it will take place.

Interestingly, there's room for webinars occurring periodically, to get this done, click on the Recurring webinar bar, you then get to decide how often it will occur, the time it should take place, and also the date when it should end.

Additional checkmates can be introduced to streamline your audience. Having a period when your audience is expected to register before a set deadline and then given a password that grants them access to the webinar via the specified gadget, you also reserve the right to decide if the host/hosts can be seen during the webinar.

Furthermore, you can choose to create opportunities for questions and answers, if the option is enabled, attendees can get to see the questions, or it's made anonymous

To access the webinar Q&A settings, scroll to Webinar Option, click Q&A, and select Schedule

Alternative hosts have the permission to oversee meetings in your stead once they receive the link via a notification email however scheduling of meetings is your responsibility.

You can save this event to your Google calendar using the confirmation page. Towards the end of the confirmation page, you'll see an invitation bar that enables you to incorporate your panelists, feed them with details of the event that are disseminated to your attendees From the email settings tab, you can determine the arrangement of emails to be sent to panelists and attendees before the event as reminders and as follow-up messages when the event is over. You can decide to add flavor to your zoom webinar by adding colorful logos/designs to invitations sent to your attendees

REGISTERING ATTENDEES FOR ZOOM WEBINAR

Under Invite Attendees, click edit. You can ask your attendees to register using a form or submit their biodata {name and email address}. Approval can be done manual or otherwise automatic

Your choice of registration should depend largely on your intention, if you have plans to follow your attendees up after the webinar/do a survey, you can ask questions that will enable you to know more about them

How to register attendees for a Zoom webinar with JotForm:

After setting up your webinar, locking down your co-hosts, it remains pertinent to get people to attend your event; hence you have to make sure attendees signing up do this without glitches

This is where Jotform comes in. It provides a glitch-free way of extracting data from attendees and it enables you to fashion the questions to suit your taste. It also allows you to sell your company value/culture through making customized designs in the form off course although templates are available, and it gives you the leverage to determine to an extent the response intended from your attendees

During the registration, attendees can be asked for relevant information such as their occupation, company name, address; it can be made compulsory before attendees sign up for your webinar

Once the attendees complete the filling of the form, they are verified automatically. This form can also be linked to several online payment platforms hence registration fees can be collected for these webinars. There are no hidden charges; hence only standard charges apply to these payment platforms are deducted

If you chose the option of automatic approval, you can just take a chill pill and watch your attendee base surge but if you opted for manual approval, you have to log in to the zoom app and manually approve those that filled the Jotform

How to enable registration for a Zoom webinar

To ensure people register, enable the register bar which is found under the personal section of your zoom portal and the webinar tab, this cannot be overemphasized and should be credence even before data collection, however, if the webinar has already been scheduled, it can be edited by selecting the already archived webinar under the 'Upcoming webinar' tab

Towards the end of the page, select Edit this Webinar, this takes you back to the menu where you can enable registration ab-initio.

HOW TO USE ZOOM FOR ONLINE MEETINGS

Online meetings are sometimes used interchangeably with Webinars. No doubt, similarities exist but there are also differences between the two

Webinars are designed to accommodate a larger group of people as opposed to an online meeting where there are usually fewer participants

Online meetings are more collaborative and give the participants a great deal of control; there's the freedom to screen-share, deliberate on matters arising whereas in webinars, opinions are aired through question and answer, only the host/ co-hosts are the ones that do the talking.

Going into the nitty-gritty, let's talk about how to use Zoom for online meetings

To help you out, here's a step-by-step guide to using Zoom Meetings the right way.

We'll cover the steps for both desktop and mobile platforms on:

- How to Set Up a Zoom Meeting
- How to Join a Zoom Meeting
- How to Schedule Meetings
- How to Record Meetings
- How to Set Up a Zoom Meeting

Here's a step-by-step guide to set up a Zoom meeting easily:

For Desktop

To start a zoom meeting, log in to your zoom account, select the 'Host a meeting' tab, the following options will surface: With Video on, With Video off, and screen share only, choose the appropriate option You will be redirected to the zoom app where the meeting can start, here you can take note of the invitation URL that attendees will need to gain access to the meeting.

To invite your participants, select the Invite button in the new meeting screen. You get the option of inviting your participants using a URL or Invitation, this can be sent via an instant message, email, or text An email containing the meeting details can be sent to the participants via your chosen email client

For Mobile Devices

Log into your zoom app, click the 'New meeting' icon, edit the meeting settings in line with the options that suit you. After that, click on the 'Start a Meeting' button. To add participants, tap the 'Participants' icon once the meeting starts, once the participant menu opens up, select the Invite tab. Then, you can share the meeting details through email, text, instant messages

HOW TO JOIN A ZOOM MEETING

You can join using a meeting link or a meeting ID

Join Using a Meeting Link

To join using a meeting link, click on the link or if using a web browser, copy and paste

Join Using A Meeting ID

Log into your zoom app, select the Join button, input the meeting ID and your display name for the meeting, tap the 'Join' button

You can now start your meeting with your partners

HOW TO SCHEDULE MEETINGS

Important meetings can be forgotten when you have a tight schedule With Zoom, however, you can schedule meetings beforehand to avoid this. This can be done by setting its date and time, providing a meeting ID, ascertaining whether it needs a password to join or not. The steps to scheduling meetings are hereby laid down:

For Desktop

Go to the zoom app and tap on the 'Schedule button'. Next, you input the meeting details in the 'Schedule meeting' icon that appears. Its data and time, privacy, and access setting can be inputted.

When you're done making adjustments, tap the schedule button at the bottom right of the screen

For Mobile

Log into the Zoom app, go to the meet and chat page, and select Schedule. Input the meeting name, time, and date, then tap done. You can save this to your calendar as a reminder

HOW TO RECORD ZOOM MEETINGS

This feature allows you to document meetings in virtual form and it's indispensable in groups who use zoom as their major tool for communication

These recordings can be saved to your device or Zoom cloud where every member of the team can access it

Here's how to record Zoom meetings:

For Desktop

Once the meeting starts, click on the 'Record' icon, you'll have two options, to record on the computer or to record to the cloud, to stop the recording, simply click on Pause/stop recording, alternatively, ending the meeting automatically stops the recording. After the meeting, the recording can be saved to your preferred storage and archived where it can be retrieved at any point in time.

For Mobile

On mobile devices, Zoom lets you save meeting recordings only to the Zoom Cloud. Here's how to record a Zoom meeting from your mobile: Here, you only have the option of saving recordings to zoom cloud. Once the meeting starts, click on the 'More' option, select the

'Record to the cloud' to begin recording, you can pause or stop recording by tapping the 'More' button, after the meeting, the recording is saved to the folder 'My Recordings.

SCHEDULING A WEBINAR

To schedule a Zoom webinar, you will need to sign in to the web interface and then go to the Webinars section and click on **Schedule a Webinar**.

- **Description** – If you want to add a description of what your webinar will be covering then you can do so here.
- **When** – This is the start date of the webinar.
- **Duration** – This is how long the webinar is scheduled to run. You can end it early or have it run longer if needed.
- **Time Zone** – If you need to change the time zone to something different than what your computer is set to then you can do so here. If you check the box for **Recurring webinar** then you will be able to schedule your webinar to re-run at specific times using the same webinar ID.
- **Webinar Password** – You can require your participants to enter a password to get into your webinar if you are concerned about security.
- **Video** – Here you can decide if you want your participant's video to automatically start when they enter your room.
- **Webinar Options** – There are several additional options you can choose from here to fine-tune your webinar experience.

- **Q&A** – This allows attendees to ask questions during the webinar that can be answered by the panelists, co-hosts, and the host.

- **Enable Practice Session** – This allows you and your panelists to get set up and familiarized with the Zoom webinar controls before you go live with your webinar.

- **Only authenticated users can join** – If you want to make your account more secure then you can set up authenticated users in your account management and then only those who have been configured will be able to join your webinars.

- **Record the webinar automatically** – Use this option if you want Zoom to record your webinar automatically without you needing to start it manually.

Once you have configured all of your webinar options then click the Schedule button to have the webinar listed in your upcoming webinars.

TEMPLATES

If you have spent some time configuring your webinar to get it just the way you like it then you might want to consider saving it as a template so you can use it over again for another webinar.

To save a current webinar as a template simply go to the settings for that webinar and click on the link that says **Save this webinar as a template**. Then you can give the template a name and decide if you would like to save the recurrences of the webinar within the template. Once you name the template click on the **Save as Template** button to have it saved to your Zoom account. Now when you go to your **Webinar Templates** under Webinars in the web interface you will see your newly saved template that you can then click on and use to schedule a new webinar using its saved settings.

BRANDING

Branding is a way to customize your webinar experience by adding things such as banners, logos, and themes to your webinar that enhances the overall look and feel of your presentation.

You can start the branding process by going to the webinar section, selecting a webinar, and then clicking the Branding section.

The various options in the Branding section and then show some examples.

Title – This information will be displayed at the top middle section of the page.

Banner – You can create your custom banner and save it as an image file to be used in your webinar.

Logo – If you have a company logo that you want to have displayed during your webinar then you can upload it from here.

Speakers – Many times you will have additional people who will be speaking during your webinar. You can upload their photo and additional information about these people in this section.

Theme – Zoom offers several different color schemes that you can choose from if you want to change the way your overall webinar looks.

Post Attendee URL – This section can be used to add a website for your company or that your attendees can go to for additional information about whatever you might be discussing in your webinar.

Post Webinar Survey – If you use any type of survey site and have set up a survey about your webinar then you can add the site address here.

Social Media Share Description – Here you can enter the description that you would like to be included when the webinar is shared on Facebook or LinkedIn and also decide if you want to include your uploaded logo or banner.

I have gone through the above settings and did things such as add a banner, logo, speaker, and post attendee URL. You will see how these apply to my webinar when it's time to start it.

CONFIGURING POLLS

Polls are a great way to get information from your attendees by asking them a question or series of questions about your webinar. You can choose from a single choice answer or a multiple-choice answer.

To get to the poll settings, simply go to your webinar and then the **Polls** section and click the **Add** button and add a question. Next, you will need to select if you want to use a single choice question or a multiple-choice question. I will use a multiple-choice question for my example and ask if anyone is interested in buying my book after hearing about it in my webinar and give them three answers to choose from.

Conclusion

Now that you have learned everything about Zoom you can now start using it in your online classes or online meetings, especially now that we are avoiding going out and meeting other people due to the going ongoing pandemic, Zoom is a big help in solving our problems. Zoom is not just about a mere video call but has many features as well such as sharing your screen, sending a file, creating polls, a delegation of duties, muting/unmuting, keyboard shortcuts, as well as safety measures to avoid Zoom bombing. This does not only help us during these times, but we can always use this during future events that require convenience and safety. I hope that you will remember everything that was discussed here because this will be very helpful in our online classes and online meetings, don't forget to be creative by changing your virtual background and many more you can explore.

This book talks a lot about technology, but it is primarily about teaching and learning. There are many ways to teach and many ways to learn. Some modalities will be more effective in some kinds of learning than others, and within each modality, some strategies are more effective than others in preparing students with the knowledge and skills to be successful in their future lives. Technology is providing an increasingly widening variety of tools that allow teachers to create that learning experience at a distance in ways that can be equally effective in developing successful learners as classroom instruction. It is all about using these tools appropriately. But technology does not replace the teacher. Regardless of how many tools you throw at a course, its success depends upon the students' willingness and capacity to engage with the course activities. Good teachers have always known that. You as the teacher make the decisions on how the technology will be used to engage your students with the content, with you, and their classmates. In a course that combines videoconferencing and an LMS, you have the strengths of both synchronous and asynchronous tools that allow you to engage your students both during and outside of class in a variety of modes that just are not possible in the traditional classroom format alone.

The consensus of research demonstrates that distance education can be as effective in meeting learning goals as classroom-based education. It just takes more work. I am confident that this work is worth the effort, however, because with distance technologies the reach of your knowledge and skills as a teacher goes far beyond a school campus. It can span the globe, bringing together international perspectives that enrichen everyone who participates. I am confident that the deep investigation into all aspects of your course teaches you that teaching in these new modalities will expand your world too, forcing you to look at teaching and learning in new ways, perhaps improving both your distance and classroom teaching. I wish you the best on your journey ahead!

It is recommended that you keep this book handy as you go, for the time being, spending the next few months always turning back to it to revise its advice, although as you grow more and more advanced, and as Zoom gains more and more updates, you'll increasingly find a potent companion in the company's website, where you can learn all about its latest features and how to work with specific devices.

However, no matter what changes, Zoom will likely remain a socially sensitive and user-friendly application, reinforcing Eric Yuan's dream of helping young lovers look into each other's eyes without having to wait a whole month or endure a grueling 10-hour train ride. This is likely why even the free version allows you to hold a conversation for eternity when it's kept small and intimate. For those who do not need to hold massive meetings with their division or department, but just want to see the faces of their family again, Zoom still has them covered.

And yet, for those whose interests are professionally inclined, zoom carries nearly every feature you could want in delivering a compelling talk to scores of people at a time, each one of whom could be connecting from anywhere in the world.

This could be you, doing all these things, right now. Potentially for free. Whatever you decide to do from this point, I hope Zoom helps make the process easier for you, whether you're trying to land your next interview, host a long-awaited reunion or set up your own small business to stay afloat and realize your dreams.

Printed in Great Britain
by Amazon

57506606R00058